THE SONGS OF
BOUBLIL & SCHÖNBERG

18 SONGS FROM LES MISÉRABLES, MISS SAIGON, MARTIN GUERRE, THE PIRATE QUEEN, AND MARGUERITE

(with music by Michel Legrand)

ISBN 978-1-4234-4177-9

ALAIN BOUBLIL MUSIC LTD.

EXCLUSIVELY DISTRIBUTED BY

HAL•LEONARD®
CORPORATION

7777 W. BLUEMOUND RD. P.O. BOX 13819 MILWAUKEE, WI 53213

Dramatic Performance Rights controlled and licensed by
Cameron Mackintosh (Overseas) Ltd.
One Bedford Square, London WC1B 3RA England
Tel (171) 637-8866 Fax (171) 436-2683

Stock and Amateur Performance Rights are licensed by
Music Theater International, Inc.
545 Eighth Avenue, New York, New York 10018
Tel (212) 868-6668 Fax (212) 643-8465

Non-Dramatic and Concert Performance Rights are controlled by
Alain Boublil Music Ltd. and licensed by the American Society
of Composers, Authors and Publishers (ASCAP), One Lincoln
Plaza, New York, New York 10023
Tel (212) 595-3050 Fax (212)787-1381

Visit Hal Leonard Online at
www.halleonard.com

CONTENTS BY SONG

CONTENTS BY SHOW

CASTLE ON A CLOUD
from *Les Misérables*

Music by CLAUDE-MICHEL SCHÖNBERG
Lyrics by ALAIN BOUBLIL, JEAN-MARC NATEL
and HERBERT KRETZMER

There is a cas-tle on a cloud.
There is a room that's full of toys.

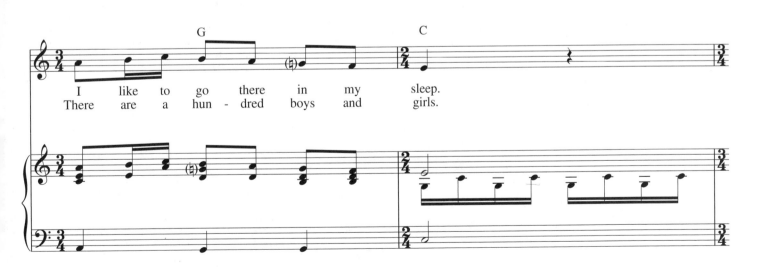

I like to go there in my sleep.
There are a hun-dred boys and girls.

CHINA DOLL
from *Marguerite*

Music by MICHEL LEGRAND
Lyrics by ALAIN BOUBLIL and HERBERT KRETZMER

THE FACE I SEE
from *Marguerite*

Music by MICHEL LEGRAND
Lyrics by ALAIN BOUBLIL and HERBERT KRETZMER

HOW DID I GET TO WHERE I AM?

from *Marguerite*

Music by MICHEL LEGRAND
Lyrics by ALAIN BOUBLIL and HERBERT KRETZMER

NOW THAT I'VE SEEN HER

from *Miss Saigon*

Music by CLAUDE-MICHEL SCHÖNBERG
Lyrics by RICHARD MALTBY, JR. and ALAIN BOUBLIL
Adapted from original French Lyrics by ALAIN BOUBLIL

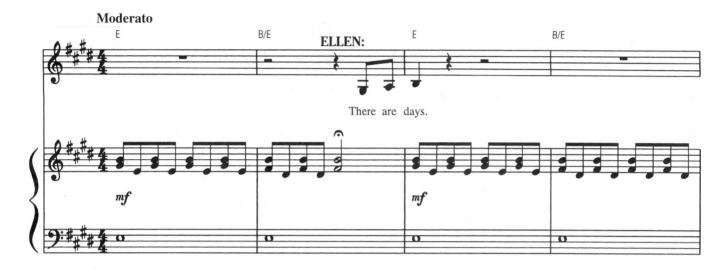

There are days.

There are days when your life clouds o-ver, and the world gets _ so

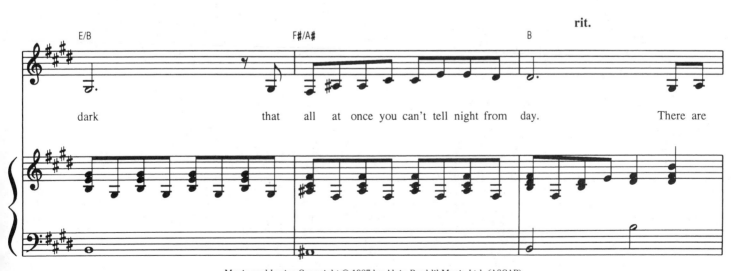

dark that all at once you can't tell night from day. There are

I know what pain her life to-day must be. But if it all comes down to

her or me, I won't wait, I___ swear_____ I'll fight.

Now that I've seen her she's

more than a name she is not some fling_ from long a-go._

Now that I've seen her I can't stay the same. Who's the man that I

al-ways trust-ed. Now I have to know._

HOW MANY TEARS?
from *Martin Guerre*

Music by CLAUDE-MICHEL SCHÖNBERG
Lyrics by ALAIN BOUBLIL and STEPHEN CLARK

on - ly to do what she feels must be right.

Some - times I won - der if some-one hears. Why must I live through

so ma - ny tears?

I DREAMED A DREAM
from *Les Misérables*

Music by CLAUDE-MICHEL SCHÖNBERG
Lyrics by ALAIN BOUBLIL, JEAN-MARC NATEL
and HERBERT KRETZMER

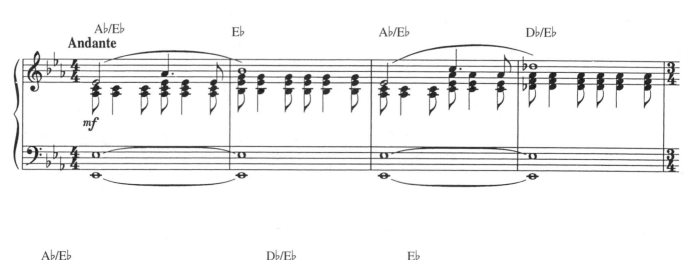

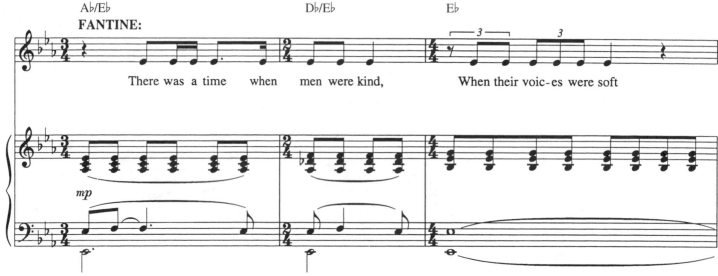

I dreamed that God would be for-giv-ing. Then I was young and un-af-

raid And dreams were made and used and wast-ed.

There was no ran-som to be paid, No song un-sung, no wine un-

tast-ed. But the ti-gers come at night

Poco piú mosso

I'D GIVE MY LIFE FOR YOU
from *Miss Saigon*

Music by CLAUDE-MICHEL SCHÖNBERG
Lyrics by RICHARD MALTBY, JR. and ALAIN BOUBLIL
Adapted from original French Lyrics by ALAIN BOUBLIL

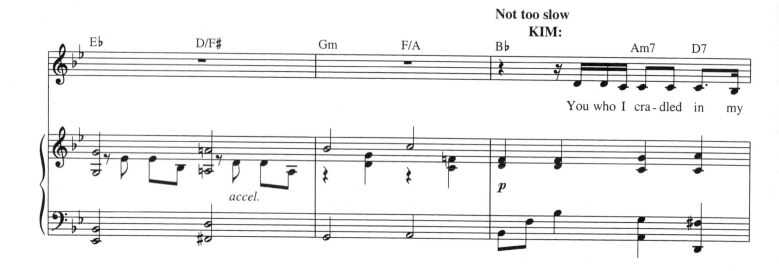

I've tast-ed love be-yond all fear.

And you should know it's love that brought you here.

Più mosso, appassionata

And in one per-fect night when the stars burned like new, I knew what I must do.

I'll give you __ a mil-lion things I'll nev-er own, I'll give you __ a world to con-quer when you're grown.

44

But there's just moon-light on my bed._____ Was he a ghost, was he a lie?__

That made my bod-y laugh and cry?___ Then by my side the proof I see:___

his lit-tle one, gods of the sun, bring him to me!_____

Tempo maestoso

You will be who you want to be. You

IN MY LIFE

from *Les Misérables*

Music by CLAUDE-MICHEL SCHÖNBERG
Lyrics by ALAIN BOUBLIL, JEAN-MARC NATEL
and HERBERT KRETZMER

This song for Cosette, Valjean, Marius and Eponine previously adapted as a solo.

THE LAST NIGHT OF THE WORLD

from *Miss Saigon*

Music by CLAUDE-MICHEL SCHÖNBERG
Lyrics by RICHARD MALTBY, JR. and ALAIN BOUBLIL
Adapted from original French Lyrics by ALAIN BOUBLIL

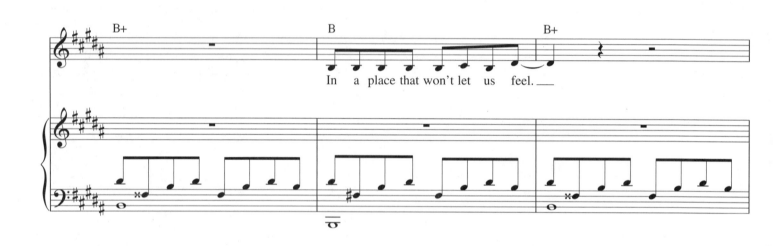

This duet for Chris and Kim has been adapted as a solo for this edition.

MON HISTOIRE
from *Les Misérables*

Music by CLAUDE-MICHEL SCHÖNBERG
Lyrics by ALAIN BOUBLIL

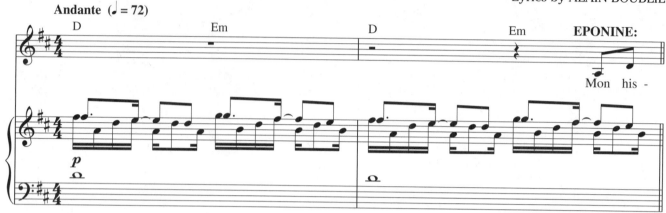

je, l'aime ____ mais comme les nuits sont cour - tes! ____ au ma-

tin, il a re - pris sa rou - te Et

le monde re - de - ve - nu le mê - me a

per - du ses cou - leurs et l'arc en ciel son di - a - dè - me Oui,

THE MOVIE IN MY MIND
from *Miss Saigon*

Music by CLAUDE-MICHEL SCHÖNBERG
Lyrics by RICHARD MALTBY, JR. and ALAIN BOUBLIL
Adapted from original French Lyrics by ALAIN BOUBLIL

This number for Gigi, Kim and Girls has been adapted as a solo for this edition.

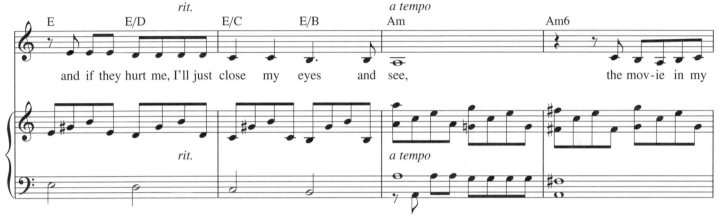

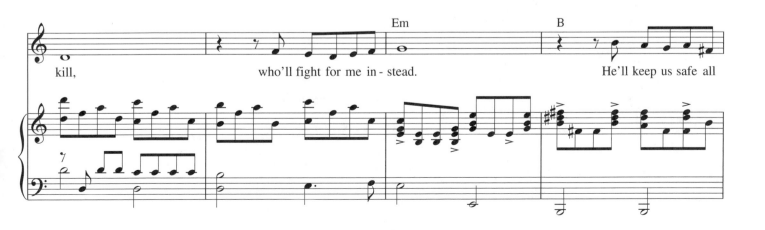

day   so no one comes at night   to blow the dream a-

way.   Dream.   The dream I have to   find.

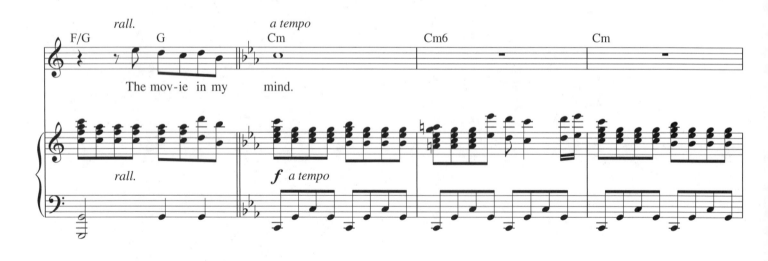

The mov-ie in my   mind.

ON MY OWN

from *Les Misérables*

Music by CLAUDE-MICHEL SCHÖNBERG
Lyrics by ALAIN BOUBLIL, JEAN-MARC NATEL,
HERBERT KRETZMER, JOHN CAIRD and TREVOR NUNN

EPONINE: And now I'm all a-lone a-gain, no-where to go, no one to turn to.

THE SEA OF LIFE
from *The Pirate Queen*

Music by CLAUDE-MICHEL SCHÖNBERG
Lyrics by ALAIN BOUBLIL, RICHARD MALTBY, JR.
and JOHN DEMPSEY

This song for Grania and Sailors has been adapted as a solo for this edition.

won't be tak - en from me!

THE WAKING OF THE QUEEN
from *The Pirate Queen*

Music by CLAUDE-MICHEL SCHÖNBERG
Lyrics by ALAIN BOUBLIL, RICHARD MALTBY, JR.
and JOHN DEMPSEY

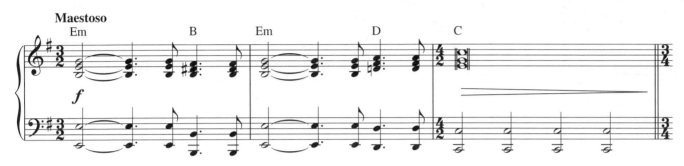

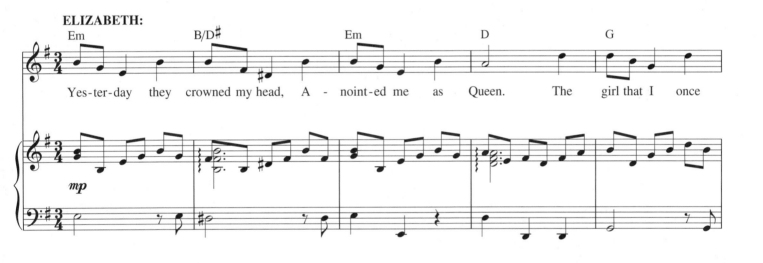

ELIZABETH:
Yes-ter-day they crowned my head, A - noint-ed me as Queen. The girl that I once

was is dead And what is here must nev-er be seen. Bring_____ our

SHE WHO HAS ALL
from *The Pirate Queen*

Music by CLAUDE-MICHEL SCHÖNBERG
Lyrics by ALAIN BOUBLIL, RICHARD MALTBY, JR.
and JOHN DEMPSEY

heart, in my hope I have more _____ than is

there.

Quasi recit.
I will car-ry on. I will not bow down to them. I will sur-vive for the day when I see once

more Both the man I love and the child I bore.

poco agitato e crescendo

see, that a wom - an in love, __ it is she, _____ who has

see, that a wom - an in love, __ it is she, _____ who has

all. _____

all. _____

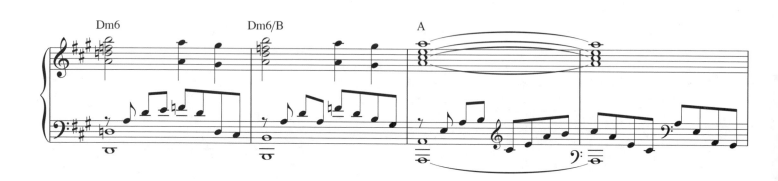

TURNING
from *Les Misérables*

Music by CLAUDE-MICHEL SCHÖNBERG
Lyrics by ALAIN BOUBLIL and HERBERT KRETZMER

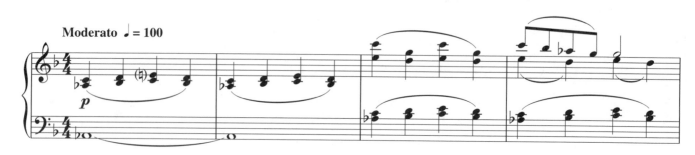

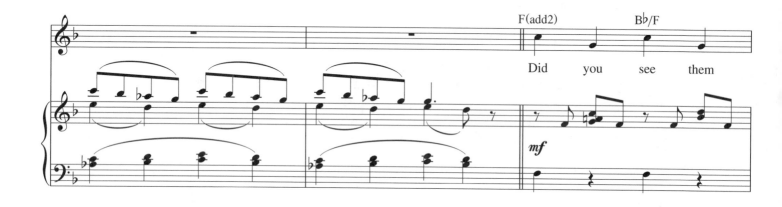

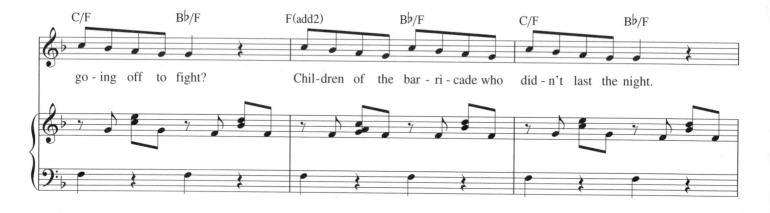

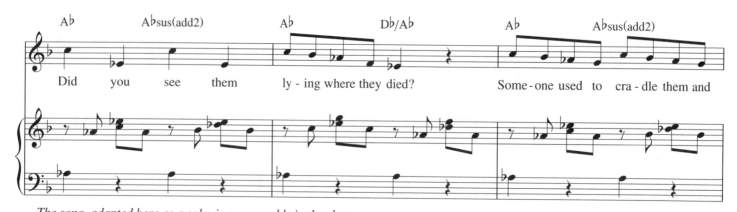

The song, adapted here as a solo, is an ensemble in the show.

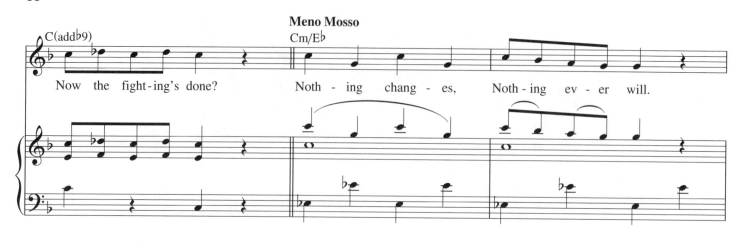

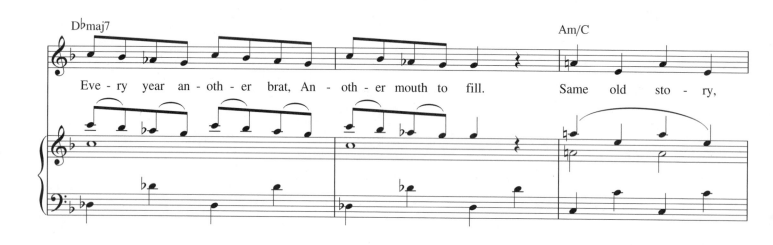

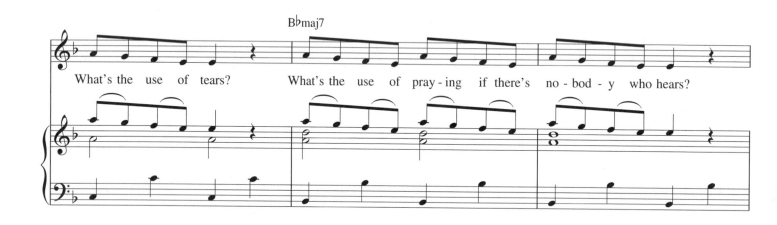

WOMAN
from *The Pirate Queen*

Music by CLAUDE-MICHEL SCHÖNBERG
Lyrics by ALAIN BOUBLIL, RICHARD MALTBY, JR.
and JOHN DEMPSEY